JO CLIFFORD

Jo Clifford is the author of over eighty works in every dramatic medium. Her work has been translated into many languages and has been performed all over the world.

Her plays include *Eve* (co-written with Chris Goode; National Theatre of Scotland); *The Tree of Knowledge* (Traverse Theatre); *Sex, Chips and the Holy Ghost* (Òran Mór); *Every One* (Royal Lyceum Theatre); *An Apple a Day* (Òran Mór/Traverse Theatre); *Losing Venice*, *Playing with Fire*, *Ines De Castro*, *Light in the Village* (Traverse Theatre); *Tchaikovsky & The Queen of Spades*, *Charles Dickens: The Haunted Man* (both for Pitlochry Festival Theatre). Also for the stage, Jo has adapted *Faust Parts 1 & 2* and *Anna Karenina* (Royal Lyceum Theatre); *Great Expectations* (Tag); *Jekyll and Hyde* (Sell A Door Productions); *La Vie De Boheme* and *Wuthering Heights*, and has translated *Schism in England*, *Life is a Dream*, *Celestina*, *The House of Bernarda Alba* and *Bintou*.

For radio, Jo has written *Spam Fritters*, *Writing Home To Mother*, *Madeleine* and *Ain't It Great To Be Bloomin' Well Dead*, and has adapted *Baltasar & Blimunda* and *The Leopard*, among many others.

Her play *The Gospel According to Jesus Queen of Heaven* has been touring Brazil for the the last two years and she will perform it over Christmas 2018 at the Traverse Theatre. Her *Five Days Which Changed Everything* has recently been broadcast on BBC Radio 3, and her *Anna Karenina* has just completed a hugely successful run in Tokyo. After performing *Eve* at Dundeee Rep, she is about to do so for the Nairn Festival and then in Brazil.

She lives in Edinburgh and is a proud father and grandmother.

For further information on Jo and her work, visit www.teatrodomundo.com.

Other Titles in this Series

Jo Clifford

LOSING
VENICE

NICK HERN BOOKS

London

www.nickhernbooks.co.uk

A Nick Hern Book

Losing Venice first published in Great Britain in 1990 by Nick Hern Books
Limited, The Glasshouse, 49a Goldhawk Road, London W12 8QP, as part of
Scot-Free

This new edition published 2018

Losing Venice copyright © 1990, 2018 Jo Clifford

Jo Clifford has asserted her moral right to be identified as the author of
this work

Cover image: www.shutterstock.com

Designed and typeset by Nick Hern Books, London
Printed in Great Britain by Mimeo Ltd, Huntingdon, Cambridgeshire
PE29 6XX

A CIP catalogue record for this book is available from the British Library

ISBN 978 1 84842 792 1

Losing Venice was first performed at the Traverse Theatre, Edinburgh, on 2 August 1985, with the following cast:

MUSICIAN/SECRETARY/ PIRATE/CONSPIRATOR ONE	Duncan Bell
MARIA/MRS DOGE/ CONSPIRATOR THREE	Carol Ann Crawford
QUEVEDO	Bernard Doherty
PABLO	Simon Donald
DUKE	Simon Dormandy
DUCHESS/ PRIEST	Kate Duchene
SISTER/CONSPIRATOR FOUR/ WOMAN WITH BABY	Irene Macdougall
KING/MR DOGE/ CONSPIRATOR TWO	Ralph Riach

Director	Jenny Killick
Designer	Dermot Hayes
Lighting and Sound	George Tarbuck

Losing Venice was revived at the Orange Tree Theatre, Richmond, on 7 September 2018, with the following cast:

PABLO	Remus Brooks
DUKE	Tim Delap
SISTER	Josh-Susan Enright
MARIA/MRS DOGE	Eleanor Fanyinka
QUEVEDO	Christopher Logan
DUCHESS/PRIEST	Florence Roberts
KING/MR DOGE	David Verrey
SECRETARY/MUSICIAN	Dan Wheeler

Pirates, conspirators and other roles played by members of the company

Director	Paul Miller
Designer	Jess Curtis
Lighting Designer	Jai Morgaria
Composer	Terry Davies
Casting Director	Annie Rowe CDG

Characters

MUSICIAN
QUEVEDO
PABLO
MARIA
DUKE
DUCHESS
SECRETARY
KING
PIRATE
PRIEST
SISTER
MR DOGE
MRS DOGE
CONSPIRATOR ONE
CONSPIRATOR TWO
CONSPIRATOR THREE
CONSPIRATOR FOUR
WOMAN WITH BABY

ACT ONE

Two benches on the stage. The audience enter to find
QUEVEDO *writing and a* MUSICIAN *playing a guitar.*
PABLO *and* MARIA *run on with a basket of food, which they*
put down in front of QUEVEDO.

QUEVEDO. What's this?

PABLO. Food.

MARIA. A picnic.

PABLO. For you.

QUEVEDO. I'm not hungry.

PABLO. Liar.

MARIA. You haven't eaten for days.

PABLO. Weeks.

MARIA. Months.

QUEVEDO. It is true I hunger but not for food.

MARIA. There. (*Exits with* PABLO.)

QUEVEDO. Bread and wine. The sacraments. The holy
  sacraments.
  We suffer hunger in a filthy world,
  Slaves to physical necessity. And yet…
  I break the bread. I drink the wine.
  Communion. Hunger is sanctified.
  I rise above the needs of the body,
  And I enter the kingdom of the soul.

  MARIA *rushes across the stage chased by* PABLO. PABLO
  is caught. MARIA *exits.*

  Pablo!

PABLO. What?

QUEVEDO. Stop it.

PABLO. What?

QUEVEDO. That.

PABLO. Why?

QUEVEDO. Because I have forbidden it.

PABLO. How?

QUEVEDO. I said I forbid it.

PABLO. You can't.

QUEVEDO. I most certainly can.

PABLO. It's my day off.

QUEVEDO. I don't care.

PABLO. Look. When I'm working I'm yours. Your beck and your call. But not now. No disrespect. (*Exits*.)

QUEVEDO. Well...
This urge to procreation I could never
understand. Two lumps of flesh.
Rubbing together. Frotting. Frot,
frot. And what, I ask, what is the
outcome? We are. What a way to start.
What a grotesque beginning. Imagine.
The slimy contact.

Enter MARIA.

MARIA. Do you mind?

QUEVEDO. Yes I do. Very much. And to do it here in public.

MARIA. Well, we can't do it in private.

QUEVEDO. You could try.

MARIA. The roof's fallen in.

QUEVEDO. The mansion of poetry is in some little disrepair.

MARIA. Have a grape.

QUEVEDO. I don't like grapes.

MARIA. Oh you do.

QUEVEDO. Not today.

MARIA. It's this wedding. Got you all upset.

QUEVEDO. I hate weddings.

MARIA. You should have been asked. That Duke. What a
   cheek. Should have invited you. And you wrote his speech
   for him, too. It's a shame.

   QUEVEDO *takes grapes*.

   There.

QUEVEDO. But these are grapes.

MARIA. True.

QUEVEDO. Pablo!

   Enter PABLO.

   These are grapes.

PABLO. Very perceptive.

QUEVEDO. You stole them.

PABLO. No, we didn't. They just happened to be there.

QUEVEDO. And the wine.

PABLO. It was hanging about.

QUEVEDO. And the knives and forks. The ducal crest.

PABLO. They just came with the wine.

QUEVEDO. If the Duke finds this we're finished. No more
   money.

PABLO. That's serious.

QUEVEDO. Yes. We can't go on like this.
   On the edge of things.
   We have got to get jobs, but if the
   Duke catches us stealing, that's it.
   The end of opportunity.
   The door closed against us forever.

PABLO. But he won't catch us, will he?

MARIA. No.

PABLO. He's busy. He's getting married.

MUSICIAN starts to play a wedding tune. He gives a malicious look to QUEVEDO, PABLO *and* MARIA *who rush to clear the food and the paper off the stage.*

Enter the DUKE *and* DUCHESS, *leading the wedding procession.*

The DUKE *looks pleased; the* DUCHESS *looks distracted. She wears spectacles,* QUEVEDO, PABLO *and* MARIA *rush back on to join the procession which has lined up centre stage. A great occasion. The* DUKE, *in sudden panic, searches for his speech.*

DUKE. Quevedo, my speech.

QUEVEDO. In your pocket.

DUKE. Thank you. My subjects. My people.
My friends. I bid you welcome.
Welcome to this hallowed place,
This seat of learning, this sacred spot,
To celebrate the joy of peace.
To consummate the power of love.
Thank you. Thank you.

Applause.

The DUKE *kisses the* DUCHESS. *She looks about for a way to wipe her mouth.* MARIA *gives a hanky to the* DUCHESS.

A touching gesture.

Quevedo. A splendid speech.

QUEVEDO. Not too long, I hope?

DUKE. Not at all, my dear fellow, not at all. But let me present you.

My bride. My poet.

QUEVEDO. Your hand is white as winter snow
but your cheeks proclaim the spring.

Your beauty makes these flowers grow
and in your hair young birds do sing.

Enthusiastic applause.

DUKE. Bravo. Bravo. But come, a feast awaits.

QUEVEDO. Honoured.

PABLO. Delighted.

MARIA. Dead chuffed.

DUKE. Your pleasure's mine. My dearest.

All leave. The DUKE *makes the* DUCHESS *stay behind.*

DUCHESS. Are you drunk?

DUKE (*on his knees*). Drunk with beauty.

DUCHESS. I was afraid so.

DUKE. Your lips like…

DUCHESS. Apples.

DUKE. Apples?

DUCHESS. Pippins.

DUKE. Is that right?

DUCHESS. Apples are red.

DUKE. Some. Not all. And your lips are red all over.

And your eyes…

DUCHESS. Like razors.

DUKE. No. Not razors. Not right. I need a poet. Quevedo!

QUEVEDO (*enters*). You called?

DUKE. I need a poem.

QUEVEDO. Did you have anything in mind?

DUKE. The beauty of women.

QUEVEDO. In general?

DUKE. The beauty of this woman.
  The joys of marriage.

QUEVEDO. Do you want something long?

DUCHESS. Make it short.

DUKE. Yes. Nothing too long.

DUCHESS. Make it a sonnet.

DUKE. Of course. A sonnet, Quevedo.

QUEVEDO. A sonnet. On the joys of marriage.

DUKE. By tomorrow morning.

QUEVEDO. Tomorrow morning.

DUKE. If you'd be so good.
  And now I must... we must, my wife and I, retire.

  Exit the DUKE *and* DUCHESS.

QUEVEDO. The marriage bed's a trough of shit.
  Fit for pigs to lie in it.

  That won't do.
  A sonnet.
  On the joys of marriage.
  Imagine.

  Enter PABLO *and* MARIA *with a bag and rolls of bedding.*
  Exit QUEVEDO, *disgusted.* PABLO *and* MARIA *survey*
  their bench.

MARIA. Is this it?

PABLO. It?

MARIA. Yes.

PABLO. Said so on the door.

MARIA. It's tiny.

PABLO. It is compact.

MARIA. Couldn't swing a cat in it.

PABLO. I don't want to swing a cat in it.

MARIA. Didn't know you were fond of animals.

PABLO. I'm not fond of animals. I had other things in mind.

MARIA. Like what, for instance?

PABLO. Bed for instance.

MARIA. You call that a bed?

PABLO. What do you call it?

MARIA. A snot rag.

PABLO. Well I've got a cold.
Look, it's better than nothing.

MARIA. It smells.

PABLO. It's got an aroma. Who cares?

MARIA. I do. Call this a castle.

PABLO. It's a palace.

MARIA. It's a pigsty.

PABLO. Look we got what we wanted. Didn't we? Well didn't we. We all got jobs. We're all in the palace.

MARIA. And look at it.

PABLO. It is a bit run-down. For a palace.

MARIA. I worked to get here.

PABLO. You didn't.

MARIA. I was nice to the Duchess.

PABLO. I thought you liked her.

MARIA. That's not the point. She owns things. And now she owns me.

PABLO. She doesn't.

MARIA. She does. Oh it's alright for you.
You don't try for anything.
You don't care. But I try.
I make an effort.

I try to get things right.
And where do I end up? Here.
It's not encouraging.

PABLO. It's a room.

MARIA. It's a hole. A dark dank hole. I want to cry.

PABLO. Don't.

MARIA. Why not?

PABLO. We could be on the street.

MARIA. You're a great comfort.

PABLO. And we're together.

MARIA. Yes. We're together.

PABLO. And all we got to do is cuddle up and forget all about it.

MARIA. We deserve better.

PABLO. We all deserve better. Everyone does. Everyone in the
whole wide world. But it's alright. It doesn't matter.

MARIA. Doesn't it?

PABLO. No, not a duchess. Not a mushroom. Not a mousehole.
Not a louse. Sssshhh.

They cuddle down. QUEVEDO *comes on with papers, which
he starts to lay down on the other bench.*

QUEVEDO. What rhymes with cock? Hock. Drunken.
Shock. Stimulating. Clock. Moralistic.
It's the new dawn, you see.
Not what you think. Marriage as a new morning. Mourning.
A new death.
Funeral baked meats. Marriage tables.
Not that. No. The crowing of the cock.
Lock. Padlock. Wedlock. Hate it.
It won't do. It's not worth it.
Not even for a roof. Not even for ten roofs.

Enter the DUKE *and* DUCHESS. QUEVEDO *hastily clears
up his papers –*

Oh it's you. My lady. My lord. Well, the joys of marriage. They're coming. We progress.

Exit QUEVEDO. *The* DUCHESS *sits and starts to read.*

DUKE. Well.

DUCHESS. Yes.

DUKE. Here we are.

DUCHESS. So it seems.

DUKE. The time has come, so to speak.

DUCHESS. Apparently.

DUKE. Shall we... shall we begin?

DUCHESS. If you like.

The DUCHESS *carefully marks her place and closes her book.*

DUKE. You could help.

DUCHESS. Could I?

DUKE. Well, yes.

DUCHESS. How?

You're frightened.

DUKE. Me? Of course not. A slight tremor. An old wound.

DUCHESS. But you've fought battles. I could never do that.

DUKE. You're a woman.

DUCHESS. Not even if I were a man.

DUKE. But then you're not.

DUCHESS. Not even if I were.

DUKE. Can we get on with this?

DUCHESS. Can't we do it tomorrow? It's been a long day.

DUKE. No.

DUCHESS. But it has.

DUKE. Yes. No we can't do it tomorrow. We must do it today.

DUCHESS. Must we?

DUKE. We are married.

DUCHESS. Yes. I don't see the connection.

DUKE. You don't?

DUCHESS. I was brought up by nuns.

DUKE. Nuns?

DUCHESS. Poor Clares.

Enlighten me.

DUKE. Certain things are expected of us.

DUCHESS. I see.

DUKE. Yes. Yes, you see the family. There is a ceremony. They are waiting for issue.

DUCHESS. Where from?

DUKE. They will look at the sheet.

DUCHESS. What for?

DUKE. Blood.

DUCHESS. But it's not my time.

DUKE. No no no. Not that sort of blood.

DUCHESS. I don't understand.

DUKE. And that damn poet's in bed!

DUCHESS. Shall I ring for him?

DUKE. No!

DUCHESS. A servant?

DUKE. No. We have to do this ourselves.

DUCHESS. But you are a duke.

DUKE. It makes no difference.

DUCHESS. Your palace is huge.

DUKE. Yes. Yes it is big.

DUCHESS. Miles of corridors.

DUKE. Forty-four miles. We had them measured.

DUCHESS. Astonishing.

DUKE. Yes. Longer than the other Dukes'. Longer than anyone's. Except the King, of course.

DUCHESS. Empty.

DUKE. Sorry?

DUCHESS. Your house. Very empty.

DUKE. But not in the old days. It was full of people then.

Horses and servants and relations. Fodder and saddles and spurs. And soldiers of course. A whole regiment of foot.

Those were the great days.

DUCHESS. Where did they all go?

DUKE. To the war, of course. Great days.

Look can we get on with this? We are married.

DUCHESS. What of it?

DUKE. Well, love.

DUCHESS. Love?

DUKE. I thought it was expected.

DUCHESS. Is there anything in your life that's unexpected?

DUKE. I should hope not. I try to be correct. Straightforward in all things but strategy.

DUCHESS. Strategy?

DUKE. In battle. The secret of success is to take the enemy by surprise. If he expects you in the front, attack him in the rear. If he expects a retreat, attack. If he expects an attack, retreat. Or else attack. So, were you a city under siege...

DUCHESS. But I'm not.

DUKE. No. More's the pity. It would be easier.

I'm sorry. I'm boring you.

DUCHESS. Not at all.

DUKE. We have a little in common.

DUCHESS. A contract.

DUKE. I was hoping some day it would be more. A little one.

DUCHESS. A little contract?

DUKE. Look if we did it now it would be over.

DUCHESS. There is that to be said for it.

DUKE. Yes.

DUCHESS. But if you did it now you might want to do it again.

DUKE. No. Never again. I promise. On my honour. As a
soldier. We must think of it as a duty. (*Points to the*
DUCHESS*'s spectacles.*) Please take these off.

DUCHESS. I can't see without them.

DUKE. That's how I like you.

DUCHESS. I've changed my mind.

The DUCHESS *evades the* DUKE *and rings a bell.* PABLO
and MARIA *sit up abruptly.*

PABLO. Oh fuck.

MARIA. We can't.

PABLO. Why not?

MARIA. That bell.

PABLO. What do we do?

MARIA. Answer it I suppose.

PABLO. You go.

MARIA. No you.

PABLO. Won't be for me.

MARIA. How do you know?

PABLO. Men don't ask for things.

MARIA. Oh don't they?

PABLO. Not at night. Anyway I don't know the way.

MARIA. Oh alright.

Why's it always me?

MARIA *crosses over to the* DUKE *and* DUCHESS.

You rang?

DUCHESS. Yes.

DUKE. Well you've got her. Tell her what you want.

DUCHESS. I need…

DUKE. Yes?

DUCHESS. A hairpin.

DUKE *and* MARIA. A hairpin?

DUCHESS. It's a custom. A well-known custom. In the south.

MARIA. I'm sorry. I come from the north.

DUCHESS. Of course you wouldn't know. The bride must always lie beside a hairpin. The touch of steel. Wards off the evil eye.

MARIA (*holding out hairpins*). A small one or a large one?

DUCHESS. I wonder.

DUKE. What are you talking about?

MARIA. I'd say large.

DUCHESS. Would you?

MARIA. I remember now. In the mountains they always say large. And very sharp in case the devil comes.

DUCHESS. These superstitions. So quaint. One should always keep up with them don't you think? I think that one. It looks sharper. There. Now we're well protected. Thank you, Maria.

You may go.

Exit MARIA.

DUKE. Thank God for that. At last.

DUCHESS. I feel safer now.

DUKE. Dammit it's gone.

DUCHESS. Where?

DUKE. So much for courtesy. So much for consideration.
I should never have waited.

DUCHESS. Something wrong?

DUKE. My sword rusts in my sheath.

DUCHESS. So sorry.

DUKE. My flank has been subdued.

DUCHESS. Then we must retire.

DUKE. A tactical retreat, I do assure you.

DUCHESS. Of course.

DUKE. I shall prepare a new assault.

DUCHESS. I await your battery with interest. Goodnight.

DUKE. Goodnight.

Exit the DUKE *and* DUCHESS.

QUEVEDO *and* MARIA *come on and meet each other.*

QUEVEDO. Yurrchh.

MARIA. Sorry?

QUEVEDO. Petrarch. He's got a lot to answer for, inventing the
sonnet. Hope he's in hell. Reading them all.

MARIA. Are you alright?

QUEVEDO. No. I'm lost. (*Shows* MARIA *half-completed poem.*)
Just before the final couplet. The darkness before the dawn.

Exit QUEVEDO.

MARIA (*moves over to* PABLO, *who has meanwhile been
masturbating*). I'm off. Pablo!

PABLO (*embarrassed*). Yes.

MARIA. Your hand's wet.

PABLO. Yes.

MARIA. And sticky.

PABLO. Yes.

MARIA. Couldn't you wait?

PABLO. I was lonely.

MARIA (*pushing him off the bench*). You idiot. You stupid selfish idiot.

PABLO. I couldn't help it.

MARIA (*picking up luggage, ready to go*). You could so.

PABLO. What did she want anyway?

MARIA. A hairpin. (*Exits.*)

PABLO. A hairpin? (*Exits.*)

    The DUKE *cries out in pain from offstage. Enter*
    QUEVEDO *and then the* DUKE, *limping. He carries a*
    dispatch case.

QUEVEDO. It's finished. Fourteen lines, six rhymes, three puns and an extended image. And on time. Your Grace. Your poem.

DUKE. The joys of marriage? Later, Quevedo. They've been postponed.

QUEVEDO. I'm sorry.

DUKE. Sorry? Ha. Quevedo, sit. Are you my friend? Even a duke must have a friend. Sit, sit.
Women, Quevedo. Women. What are they for? What use are they? What function do they serve?

QUEVEDO. The ancients found uses for them.

DUKE. And have we progressed no further?
Must we continue to be enslaved?
Why did I get married?

To get a son, Quevedo. A son.
It is most unfortunate.
Why is there no other way?

QUEVEDO. Plato believed –

DUKE. Plato. That upstart. My line, Quevedo, stretches back to
the Goths. The glorious Goths. Is it to die? Can it not stretch
forward to the... the...

QUEVEDO. The future.

DUKE. Yes. Thank you. The future. But not even there can she
be trusted. God knows, she might even spawn a daughter.

QUEVEDO. It is possible.

DUKE. Possible? Quevedo, if only she were a man. She would
understand the necessity. We would talk it over, like sensible
people, agree on what had to be done. And then we would do
it. Whatever was necessary. And then it would be over. All
over. We could have a drink and be friends. But with her.

Tears. Recriminations. Contradictions. A painful scene.

QUEVEDO. You're limping.

DUKE. It's nothing. Nothing. An old wound. Gained in war.
A source of pride.

Oh it is peace, Quevedo, peace that
underlies our ills. Peace. A woman's
invention. Peace rots the soul.
Spain was not made for peace.
Spain's greatness was forged in war.
Our empire built on the blade of a sword.
Several swords. A hundred.
Several hundred thousand swords.

QUEVEDO. That now rust.

DUKE. Precisely. Rust. Rot with disuse.
You see the people? Look at them.
Decaying in idleness.
They lead such hopeless, senseless lives.
No aspiration beyond riches. No direction.
They need a purpose, Quevedo. To take

them outside their lives.
And where will they find it? In war.
Ask any man still old enough to remember.
Ask them of the times they felt alive.
They will tell you: it was in the war.
That was when they had purpose.
That was when they lived. Our duty is
plain. To bring an end to peace.

QUEVEDO. I had not known you were at peace.

DUKE. Precisely. Enemies surround me.
Leeches tug at my heels.

QUEVEDO. Dogs.

DUKE. I beg your pardon?

QUEVEDO. At your heels. Dogs.

DUKE. Yes dogs. They suck me dry.
The usurers are at my back and I am
helpless. Helpless. My hands are tied.
It takes a bold stroke, Quevedo, to turn
upon the snivelling rats and drive them
backwards. Will you join me?

QUEVEDO. Me?

DUKE. Are you content to scribble poems, indulge in your
fantastic theories?

QUEVEDO. My fantastic theories?

DUKE. Isn't that what you do, you poets?

QUEVEDO. We write poems.

DUKE. And who reads them? Forgive me if I talk frankly. No
doubt your work is much admired. So people tell me, people
who know such things. But this country. This country we so
dearly love, is she admired? She used to be. She used to be
great, used to be respected, used to be feared. But now what
part do we play in the world?

We apologise. It is not worthy of us. I sense in you a great
impatience. Will you join me? Are you with me?

QUEVEDO. I have always been with you. In spirit.
    I watched you, striding through the fields of Flanders
    Dealing out death on the Italian mountains.
    I was with the vultures, glorying in the downfall of our
    enemies.
    But what became of your victories?
    They slipped away like grains of sand.

DUKE. A tragedy. Lost opportunities.
    Peace undoes all that war achieves.
    Fudge and mudge, Quevedo.
    Disgraceful compromise.
    Where is the scope for resolution?
    We belong to a nation of pygmies.
    Men of straw totter across the public
    stage, posturing and mouthing. Dummies.

QUEVEDO. Spain is sick. I watch her agony on the sidelines.
    Words. Words.
    I am tired of words.

DUKE. Do not underestimate the power of words.
    We have great men on our side, Quevedo,
    Men of the greatest courage and resolution,
    But we have problems.
    The problem of communication.
    People do not understand.
    Once in Italy we came upon a house.
    It stood right in the enemy's line of fire.
    A sitting target for their cannons.
    And so of course we burnt it.
    What else could we do?

    There was a lull in the fighting,
    Women, old men crawled about in the wreckage.
    Don't weep, I told them, we did it for you.
    Your house is safe. We have saved it.
    But they would not believe.
    You see, I speak so badly.
    But had you been there, you with your gift for words…

    But enough talk. Time for action.
    We must act swiftly. We cannot wait for agreement, we must
    act from conviction.

But there is danger. Ignoble as it is
I too, have learnt to conspire.
And now I have the ears of the King.
Here. In this dispatch case.

QUEVEDO. Are you sure?

DUKE. One can never be sure. I think, I suspect, I surmise.
I can say no more. For now we are surrounded by spies. But
I can tell you this: I am setting in train a foreign adventure.
The King is sick, but I have access to his secretary. I go to
seek him now. Farewell.

QUEVEDO. Farewell?

DUKE. Trust me, Quevedo. Together we shall change the world.

QUEVEDO. But my poem…

DUKE. You still care about your poem? Then write me another.
The treachery of women, the futility of love. For this
evening. Read it to my wife. We will surprise her. Farewell.
(*Exit* DUKE.)

QUEVEDO. He's mad. What of it? Power is madness.
The world is corrupt. Action is futile.
Love is a farce. Happiness, impossible.
Poetry the only meagre consolation.
To work, Quevedo. Destroy happiness. (*Exit* QUEVEDO.)

Enter the DUCHESS *and* MARIA *with a basket.*

DUCHESS. Is this the place? We'll just say it is, shall we? And
if anyone complains, we'll just tell them we didn't know.
We'll say we weren't told.

MARIA. It's nice here, anyway.

DUCHESS. Must be the one pleasant spot in the whole place.
Must be a mistake. Oh, Maria, what shall I do?

You know what we're supposed to do?
We're supposed to take the sheet and hang it up where
everyone can see it. They say it makes the ground fertile.
And it has to happen at noon. And why does it have to
happen at noon? Because it's always happened at noon. And
why does it have to be this basket? Because it's always been

this basket. That's all this basket's for. The basket of the
Virgin's blood.

It's like everything else. It's there because it always has
been. They do it because they always have. That's why it's
such a great house, Maria, that's why it's stood so long.
That's why it's so dark that's why it's so full of dust. That's
why it's so damp that's why it's so cold. That's why I can't
breathe in it.

Oh, Maria, what shall I do? I shouldn't have married him.
I knew it was a mistake. Have you got a hanky? Men, Maria.
What's the use of them? What possible function do they
serve? What conceivable benefit are they to any part of the
world? Well? Can you think of any?

MARIA. Don't we need them?

DUCHESS. Whatever for?

MARIA. Children?

DUCHESS. I wonder. My father had precious little to do with
me. He just did the one thing, the one thing he couldn't get
out of, and then he died. And all his money went into trust.
Every penny of it. He gave it all to some lawyer so I
wouldn't get it until I married. And now I am married who
gets it? My husband. The Duke. It isn't right and it isn't fair
and I can't do a thing about it.

MARIA. There must be something.

DUCHESS. Well I can't think what. Are they all like him? Men?
I haven't met that many. Thank God. He's so boring. Not
what I expected at all. Not what I dreamed of. You know,
Maria, when I was a girl you know what I did? I ran away.
I crept out one night when no one was looking. I'd read all
these books about knights in armour and I wanted… I wanted
an adventure. I think I wanted to meet St George. I never did.
They brought me home on a mule. And here I am. And
what'll I do?

MARIA. I wish I knew.

DUCHESS. We'll think of something. Shall we? Anyway. Is your
room nice?

MARIA. No.

DUCHESS. And mine's horrid too. We'll have to do something.
We'll just have to get rid of him, that's all. You know
anything about poison? Neither do I. I don't think I could use
it anyway. I'd be too nervous. Put it in the wrong glass. Why
can't he go to war? He's very good at war. Are there any?

MARIA. I don't know.

DUCHESS. Where could he go? Somewhere distant.
Somewhere impossibly remote. London, for instance.

MARIA. Where?

DUCHESS. You're right. Who'd ever want to go there.
Anyway, how could we send him?

MARIA. Couldn't someone else?

DUCHESS. Maria, you're brilliant. I know someone who could
do it. Writes letters for the King. Someone terribly important.
I'll ask him. I'll go this minute.

MARIA. But you can't.

DUCHESS. Oh, the sheet. I was forgetting.

MARIA. There's people coming.

DUCHESS. But what'll we do?

MARIA. You take one end.

DUCHESS. Yes.

MARIA. And I take the other.

DUCHESS. You're right. Oh, Maria. Shh. Here they come.

Music. Enter all the cast, in procession, the DUKE *leading.*
They pass ceremonially under the sheet, turn round, applaud
it. Confetti.

MARIA *and the* DUCHESS *fold up the sheet and join them*
as they process offstage. QUEVEDO *stays behind and*
prepares to write.

QUEVEDO. Pablo!

PABLO (*enters*). Yes.

QUEVEDO. I want paper.

PABLO. Paper?

QUEVEDO. Reams of it. Mountains of it.

PABLO. Coming.

QUEVEDO. Cut down the forests and bring them to my desk.

PABLO. This enough?

QUEVEDO. And lakes of ink.

PABLO. Lakes?

QUEVEDO. No oceans. The wide storm-tossed seas.

PABLO. Give us a minute.

QUEVEDO. And a flock of pens, Pablo, a cloud of whitened
  wings.

PABLO. You want pens.

QUEVEDO. Goose pens, Pablo.

PABLO. Goose pens.

QUEVEDO. Flying over the inky waters
  and burying their heads in the depths
  for food.
  Then let them vomit on the paper to
  their hearts' content.

PABLO. Yes.

QUEVEDO. I'm thinking of ducks. No matter.

PABLO (*hassled*). No.

> QUEVEDO *settles down to write. Enter* MARIA.

MARIA. How's it going?

PABLO. Terrible!

MARIA. Oh.

PABLO. People keep shouting at me.

MARIA. Oh. Poor thing.

PABLO. I can't get a minute's peace.

MARIA. Things are fine for me.

PABLO. Are they?

MARIA. The Duchess is really nice.

PABLO. You watch her. She'll be up to something.

MARIA. She's not like that.

PABLO. They're all the same.

MARIA. I think I'm going to like it here.

PABLO. I know I'm going to hate it.

MARIA. Oh, Pablo. It won't be for long.

PABLO. Oh won't it.

MARIA. She'll set me up. She said she would. Well, she almost did. Just think. A place of our own. A little shop. What'll we sell?

PABLO. Fish.

MARIA. Ugh. Not fish. Something nice. Bread. I love the smell of bread. And those sticky cakes.

PABLO. Lot of work.

MARIA. I'd stay up all night, baking. And when I got tired I'd just look up at the stars. And when dawn came I'd give children the pieces of hot crust and the loose ends of fresh pies. I'd spend the morning handing out this lovely food.

We'd make love all afternoon and in the evening I'd go to sleep.

PABLO. You'd put chalk in the flour.
You'd paint the crusts brown.
You'd buy the flour cheap and you'd sell the bread dear.
You'd drive beggars from your door with dogs.

MARIA. Am I that cruel?

PABLO. It's not you, love. It's the world. No one's honest in the world.

MARIA. But you are.

PABLO. Me? I steal things.

MARIA. That doesn't stop you being honest.

PABLO. Doesn't stop me being poor.

MARIA. Everyone's poor.

PABLO. Except the rich.

MARIA. Everyone who matters. And – (*Makes a rude noise.*) the rich.

PABLO (*makes a rude noise*). The rich? Nah – (*Makes a ruder noise.*) them.

Both make ruder and ruder noises. QUEVEDO *interrupts. He's finished his poem.*

QUEVEDO. That's it. The end. It's all over.
Human happiness? Denied.
Marital bliss? Ridiculed.
The joys of love? Negated.
And in blank verse.

Rude noises from PABLO *and* MARIA.

Oh, go away.

Exit PABLO *and* MARIA. QUEVEDO *calls out after them.*

No more marriages. An end to fornication.
No more births. No more squealing monsters.

A huge fart offstage. Enter the DUKE.

DUKE. Quevedo! The King will see us.

QUEVEDO. But my poem.

DUKE. Your poem?

QUEVEDO. Yes, my poem!

DUKE. Later, Quevedo.

QUEVEDO. Later?

DUKE. Don't fret. Write another. For the King.

QUEVEDO. The majesty of state?

DUKE. Yes.

QUEVEDO. The generosity of ministers?

DUKE. Of course.

QUEVEDO. The glory of the garden!

DUKE. Yes! An ode, Quevedo. An ode. As long as you like.
But don't be late.

He scatters QUEVEDO*'s papers, and leaves.*

QUEVEDO (*furious*). Pablo!

Enter PABLO. QUEVEDO *bashes him with a roll of paper.*

PABLO. More paper?

QUEVEDO. I've got too much. Take it away.

PABLO (*clearing up scattered paper*). Only trying to help.

QUEVEDO. Then help me.

PABLO. What with?

QUEVEDO. I've got to praise a king.

PABLO. That's your job.

QUEVEDO. Praising marriage was bad enough. This is worse.
I don't want to do it. I'm tired.

PABLO. Then go to bed.

QUEVEDO. I can't. All I know is words. They paper over
hollow spaces.

PABLO. Then let them.

QUEVEDO, *furious, is about to attack* PABLO. *Enter the*
DUKE.

DUKE. The King will see us now.

They line up. Enter SECRETARY, *with papers.*

Let me present you. The ears of the King. His secretary. My poet.

QUEVEDO. Honoured.

SECRETARY. At your service. And this?

QUEVEDO. My squire.

SECRETARY. I see. As the King approaches you will kneel.

You are not to die. Be grateful. You will remove these.

QUEVEDO (*takes off spectacles*). But I can't see without them.

SECRETARY. So much the better. The King is not to be seen.

He is to be feared. You will see nothing. Hear nothing. Say nothing. You will approach in silence. You will not wish His Majesty health: that is no longer desirable. The King bears his cross with joy. He slept beside the corpse of the blessed Catherine. You will see the benefit. His stench, coming from a mortal, would be unbearable. From him it is incense. You will take pleasure in it. He comes. Withdraw.

Enter the KING. *He smells. The* DUKE *takes pleasure in it.*

QUEVEDO *and* PABLO *are disgusted. They retreat and await the* SECRETARY's *orders.*

SECRETARY. Your Majesty.

KING. Who are you?

SECRETARY. Your secretary.

KING. My under-secretary.

SECRETARY. Under the shadow of Your Majesty's might.

KING. Naturally. You have business with me?

SECRETARY. Indeed, Your Majesty. The...

Begins to point out the DUKE. *The* KING *forestalls him.*

KING. The Fourth Regiment of Foot?

SECRETARY (*hastily searching through his papers*). The Fifth, Your Majesty means the Fifth.

KING. And what do they want?

SECRETARY. Boots, sire.

KING. How dare they.

SECRETARY. They beg you. Humbly, Your Highness.

KING. I can hardly walk. Why should they?

SECRETARY. They are infantry.

KING. My legs rot.

SECRETARY. Your legs mature.

KING. Maggots crawl between my toes.

SECRETARY. Magnificent beasts.

KING. My confessor says I must love them.

SECRETARY. Nothing is beyond Your Highness's power.

KING. I tell him I try. I try, but there is so little time. The affairs of the state, leave little space for love.

SECRETARY. Indeed, Your Majesty. And now –

KING. Our loyal dwarfs?

SECRETARY (*looking for the document*). They beg permission to marry.

KING. Have we not dwarfs enough?

SECRETARY. The figures are not currently available.

KING. Collect them. Remit the matter to council. I trust you are not well?

SECRETARY. Indeed not, Your Majesty. My chest is stuffed with phlegm.

KING. I hate to see a man in health.

SECRETARY. Your Majesty, the matter of the Duke.

KING. Which Duke?

SECRETARY. Osuna.

KING. We have too many dukes.

SECRETARY. He wants to be sent away.

KING. Oh, does he?

SECRETARY. I received representations only yesterday.

KING. Did you? Hmmm. Is he fat?

SECRETARY. Quite thin.

KING. Dangerous.

SECRETARY. A man of determination and resolve.

KING. The worst of all. A menace to the state. You know my view: people are the bane of government. They continually get in the way. But since they must be tolerated, let them at least be docile. Activity and independence I simply cannot stand.

SECRETARY. The world trembles at Your Majesty's wrath.

KING. Good. And so. This Duke. What of him?

SECRETARY. He asks to be sent away. With his poet.

KING. There are too many poets.

SECRETARY. I was thinking of Venice.

KING. Venice... The best assassins in Europe. The deepest dungeons. Threatened by invasion and riddled with plague. Excellent, excellent. Are the papers ready?

SECRETARY. Naturally. And the subjects await your pleasure.

KING. I have no pleasure. I have only pain.

SECRETARY *gestures to the* DUKE. *The* DUKE, QUEVEDO *and* PABLO *move toward the* KING *on their knees*.

News of the dwarfs?

SECRETARY. It is the Duke, Your Highness.

KING. The Duke?

DUKE. At your service.

KING. The worms are getting fat.

DUKE. Indeed.

KING. What think you of Venice?

DUKE. Venice, Your Majesty? Er... the centre of Europe
strategically vital... menaced by the Turk...

My poet...

QUEVEDO. Venice. City of dreams. City of the sea
A city of music and secret harmonies,
Which glories in the arts of life
And has forgotten all the arts of war.
Where swords rust in their sheaths
And cannons moulder in dark corners.
Seabirds sing in the streets.
Wine flows from the fountains.
The prisons are empty.
Every door is open,
And the people have thrown away the keys.

KING. I can't find it on the map.

SECRETARY. We had it removed.

KING. Of course. It displeased us.

SECRETARY. You appreciate the position.

DUKE. Of course.

KING. Good. We appoint you governor.

Viceroy of Venice. Here are the papers.

DUKE. But it is not in our dominions.

KING. Precisely. A test for your valour. Your zeal for our cause.
We appreciate initiative.

DUKE. A chance for glory.

KING. Oh yes. Great glory.

DUKE. I accept.

KING. I will pray for your victory. (*To* SECRETARY.) To the
chapel. Conduct me. *A Te Deum.*

Exit KING *and* SECRETARY.

DUKE. Venice! Italy! The world! Our troubles are over. Our glories begin.

PABLO. Was that the King?

DUKE. Of course.

PABLO. Should be different.

DUKE. What an audience! What magnificent presence! (*To* QUEVEDO.) You seem sad.

QUEVEDO. Is this wise?

DUKE. Wisdom has nothing to do with it! This calls for resolution. And we have it. If we are together, who can stand against us?

Come. Together we will change the world.

Exit the DUKE. QUEVEDO *follows*. PABLO *hides under a bench*.

Enter MARIA.

MARIA. What's happened?

PABLO. I've got to go.

MARIA. Where?

PABLO. I don't know. I don't want to.

MARIA. Then don't go.

PABLO. I must. I've been ordered.

Enter the DUCHESS.

DUCHESS. It's worked, Maria. He's going! What's wrong?

MARIA. They're sending him away too.

DUCHESS. Oh.

Enter the DUKE *and* QUEVEDO. QUEVEDO *with arms and conquistador's helmet*.

DUKE. Congratulate me.

DUCHESS. Of course.

DUKE. Now you're sad too. What's the matter with everybody?

DUCHESS. We're sad at your going.

DUKE. Yes. I know. The women stay behind.
    The fate of war. Be strong.
    We move to higher things.
    A greater challenge. A higher glory.
    Pablo!

  PABLO *reluctantly crawls out from the bench, kisses*
  MARIA, *and falls in beside the* DUKE.

Quevedo. We have our orders.

QUEVEDO. I want to write a poem.

DUKE. It's too late. Poetry is finished.

  Words are useless. We count on action alone. Follow me.
  To Venice!

  They march off: the DUCHESS *and* MARIA *wave goodbye.*

ACT TWO

Sea noises. QUEVEDO, PABLO *and the* DUKE *sit on one bench. A* SAILOR *stands on the other. They all rock together in the gentle swell.*

Enter PIRATES *behind a door. They push it across the front of the stage, take up position, and burst through the door with a flash and a bang.*

Shrieks and yells. A fierce fight. PABLO *hides in the audience.*

QUEVEDO *and the* DUKE *are captured.*

QUEVEDO. Curious failure of the intellect, this.

PIRATE. You sound rich.

QUEVEDO. I am.

PIRATE. Good.

QUEVEDO. Rich in distinction.

PIRATE. I want gold.

QUEVEDO. Why didn't you ask?

DUKE. Don't listen to him. He's a poet.

PIRATE. And who are you?

DUKE. A duke.

PIRATE. Are you rich?

DUKE. In honour.

PIRATE. Overboard.

DUKE. Wait. You can't.

PIRATE. Want to bet?

DUKE. But I'm a duke. You hear me? A duke!

The DUKE *is forced to exit through the door.*

PIRATE. Search him.

QUEVEDO. You won't find anything. I'm a poet.
I have a finer gold. In here (*Points to head.*) Locked and
bolted.
And you don't have the key.

PIRATE. What's this? (*Takes off* QUEVEDO*'s glasses.*)

QUEVEDO. Glasses. Give them back.

PIRATE. What are they for?

QUEVEDO. Seeing. Please.

PIRATE. Can't see a thing. Useless. (*Throws them away.*)

QUEVEDO. I can't see.

PIRATE. You don't need to.

QUEVEDO. Wait. Remember Arion.

PIRATE. Why?

QUEVEDO. He was a poet, captured by pirates off
the coast of Tyre.
They stole all he had and threw him into the sea.
But, before they did, they granted him one last request.
They let him play his flute.
A dolphin, who happened to be passing,
found the notes so sweet it rescued the
poet from his watery grave and carried
him home to Tyre.
He thanked the dolphin, and then, as he
walked up the beach one day, playing
his flute, suddenly at his feet he saw a heap of gold.
He looked up and there was the dolphin.
It had swum back to the ship, stove in
its planks with one lash of its furious
tail, sunk the ship, stole the gold,
and brought it back to the poet.
The music-loving beast.
And all the wicked pirates drowned.

The PIRATES *confer.*

PIRATE. You got a flute?

QUEVEDO. No.

PIRATE. No problem. Overboard.

QUEVEDO. You can't. You need me. I'm a poet!

QUEVEDO *is forced to exit through the door. The* PIRATES *find* PABLO.

PABLO. Heard the one about the sad sea captain?
He always went out whaling. Wait.
I once knew a mate of yours.
Retired from the trade.
Went on shore, turned respectable.
Bought a bakery. But after two weeks
he burnt it down. You know why?
He wasn't happy with the pie rate.
Do you ever laugh?

About to exit, changes his mind.

There was once a dolphin, swimming sadly
in the sea. You know what made him so
unhappy? He couldn't see a porpoise in it.

Exit PABLO. *The* PIRATES *get the joke. They collect their weapons and exit through the door.* QUEVEDO *and* PABLO *crawl on, gasping.*

Lucky about the plank. Pity about the Duke.

QUEVEDO. Where are we?

PABLO. How should I know?

QUEVEDO. It smells like Venice.

PABLO. Smells like rotting fish.

QUEVEDO. Nonsense, Pablo. We're there.
Smell it. The dreaming towers.
The golden domes.
And what a journey!
I must write an epic.

PABLO. Must you?

QUEVEDO. Boreas blew our battered bark.

PABLO. Who?

QUEVEDO. Boreas. The North Wind. Wait a minute. Boreas? Boreas?

Isn't it Boreas?

PABLO. How should I know?

QUEVEDO. When Boreas blew our battered bark... This is serious.

PABLO. It's blowing from the south. (*Holds up finger.*) Look.

QUEVEDO. That's irrelevant. It was fierce, it was ferocious. It blew us off-course.

PABLO. But it was pirates.

QUEVEDO. Look, are you the poet or am I?

PABLO. Sorry.

QUEVEDO. Now I'll have to start again.

PABLO. You can't.

QUEVEDO. And why ever not?

PABLO. No paper. No pens. No ink. No Duke.

QUEVEDO. You're right. We're stuck. What'll we do?

Enter the PRIEST, *a strange and sinister figure.*

PABLO. There's someone. I'll ask.

Excuse me...

QUEVEDO. Pablo!

PABLO. What's wrong?

QUEVEDO. We're Spaniards.

PABLO. We need help.

QUEVEDO. Aren't we supposed to be secret?

PABLO. Don't worry. I'll be secret.

QUEVEDO. At least inconspicuous.

PABLO. Excuse me is this Venice?
　　Venice? Venice. Venice.
　　V-e-n-i-s. Are you deaf?
　　Blind? Deaf and blind?
　　Do you speak Spanish?

QUEVEDO. Pablo!

PABLO. Don't worry. Go and write your poem. Leave it to me.

QUEVEDO. Alright. I will. (*Goes and sits down.*)

PABLO. Oi. You. Listen. I need help.
　　Help. No speak Spanish?
　　Italian. Italiano. Help.
　　I needa help. Helpa.
　　Helpo.

The PRIEST *approaches,* PABLO *panics.*

Help. Help! Help! Help.

PABLO *faints on the bench. Music. The* PRIEST *goes over to* PABLO, *checks he's asleep, then listens to* QUEVEDO.

QUEVEDO (*in a reverie; unaware of* PRIEST). Peace. Peace.
　　Nothing happens.
　　The secret rhythms of the sea.
　　The sun sinks. And then it rises.
　　Always knows just what to do.
　　Always knows. Always.
　　The hidden harmonies.
　　Always under all this nonsense of politics.

PRIEST. Quevedo. Come.

QUEVEDO. Who are you?

PRIEST. I am a watcher by the shore.

QUEVEDO. How do you know my name?

PRIEST. I seek lost travellers.

QUEVEDO. You don't know me. No one knows me.

PRIEST. Your fame has preceded you.

QUEVEDO. I'm not famous.

PRIEST. Not famous? Quevedo the poet? Quevedo the satirist? Quevedo whose wit is a lash under which the mighty tremble? Quevedo the man of action? Quevedo the saviour of Venice?

QUEVEDO. It's not possible.

PRIEST. It is very possible. This is Venice.

QUEVEDO. It is Venice. But where is my servant?

PRIEST. Taken to a place of rest.

QUEVEDO. Have I been betrayed?

PRIEST. How could you be? This is Venice. Nothing is hidden here. All is known.

QUEVEDO. Then all is lost.

PRIEST. Nothing is lost. Now come.

QUEVEDO. Don't want to go. I want to stay here. In the sun.

PRIEST. I am offering you help.

QUEVEDO. I don't need help. Everything is normal.

PRIEST. You appear to be in trouble.

QUEVEDO. A little local difficulty perhaps. But I'll manage.

PRIEST. You will sleep.

The PRIEST *looks at* QUEVEDO. *Music.* QUEVEDO *yawns, sleeps.*

The PRIEST *moves across to* PABLO.

Enter SISTER, *with towel and basin. The* PRIEST *and* SISTER *quietly greet each other.*

The PRIEST *moves back to beside* QUEVEDO. SISTER *begins to wash* PABLO'*s feet. He wakes with a start.*

PABLO. What are you doing?

SISTER. Washing your feet.

PABLO. Don't. They're dirty.

SISTER. All the more reason to wash them.

PABLO. No one's ever washed my feet.

SISTER. Time someone did.

PABLO. You're tickling.

SISTER. There. What a fuss. Now your hands. That one first. Now this one. Your hair needs brushing.

PABLO. Am I dreaming?

SISTER. What do you think?

PABLO. I was. I dreamt I was safe. I was taken in. I was washed and dressed and laid to sleep.

SISTER. And so you were.

PABLO. And nothing was asked in return.

SISTER. This is Venice. Brush your hair.

PABLO. Why do you do this?

SISTER. This is what I do.

PABLO. All the time?

SISTER. Some of the time.

PABLO. Then who are you? May I ask?

SISTER. A sister.

PABLO. A nun? I know all about nuns. They're big and they're black and they beat you.

SISTER. Is that right?

PABLO. You're not like that.

SISTER. I hope not.

PABLO. But are you… are you…

SISTER. Chaste? Oh yes. Very chaste.

PABLO. Not the other kind.

SISTER. Is there another kind?

PABLO. At home, yes. Nunneries are just a joke. Perhaps I shouldn't say such things.

SISTER. No, Pablo. Not ever. Not here.

PABLO. Don't go. But… what else do you do?

SISTER. We pray. We study. We sing in the choir.

PABLO. Doesn't sound very interesting.

SISTER. Should it be?

PABLO. But don't you like it?

SISTER. It's hard. I don't sing well, and the services are very long.

PABLO. Then why did you come?

SISTER. I had nowhere else. Someone brought me.

PABLO. How can such things happen? It's wrong.

SISTER. It happens.

PABLO. Is there nowhere else?

SISTER. Nowhere.

PABLO. A lovely person like you. It's a waste. It's such a waste.

And you are lovely. In every way. You are. Maybe I shouldn't say it, but you are.

SISTER. Where do you want to take me?

PABLO. I never said that.

SISTER. There's no harm in wanting.

PABLO. I can't. I'd like to, but I can't.

SISTER. No harm. It may not happen, but there's no harm.

PABLO. You're right. I want to take you out. Out of here. Out to the world.

SISTER. You know all about the world?

PABLO. I get by. But you mustn't rot in here. You mustn't.

You must belong somewhere. Can't I take you?

SISTER. I lived not far from here. In a village.

PABLO. Is it nice?

SISTER. It was. I had a lover there. His name was Pablo.

PABLO. Like mine.

SISTER. He was a good man. We were going to have a child.

We were happy. Then he went away.

PABLO. Why? How could he?

SISTER. He was taken. Someone had started a war. Then soldiers came. Spaniards.

PABLO. Like me.

SISTER. You burnt my village.

PABLO. I'm sorry.

SISTER. I hid, and they never found me. They were too busy killing. But they found my friend. Marcella. She was pregnant. They split open her belly and took out the baby in front of her eyes. They called it pacification. I saw it. She was still alive. She called for water, but I couldn't give her any. Then she died. After dark I ran away. They were drunk. I hid in the graveyard. I went underground, I gave birth to my baby. I bit my lip so I wouldn't scream. I cut the cord with my teeth. I had watched the midwives. He was a boy. His eyes were blue. He looked up and laughed. The soldiers moved on. They had emptied the granaries. I found some potatoes. My child no longer smiled. He was potbellied and sickly. I went to the city. They told me we'd be safe. We found somewhere, not much, off an alley. I thought things were better. The third week, the child died. Why should I have any use for the world?

Exit SISTER. *The* PRIEST *follows.* QUEVEDO *wakes up. He sees* PABLO *and rushes across to embrace him.*

QUEVEDO. Pablo, my friend. My dear dear friend.

PABLO. I want to go home.

QUEVEDO. Listen. I've got it.

PABLO. I'm sick of this place.

QUEVEDO. The spirit of wit. The soul of poetry.

PABLO. Where have you been?

QUEVEDO. Talking with the mother.

PABLO. I never saw her.

QUEVEDO. No. No you wouldn't…
It's all graded you see.
Everything has its level. You have
yours, I have mine. Not lower, not
higher, but ordered. Perfectly
ordered. The old astronomy was right.
I know what you're going to say.
Galileo.

PABLO. Not exactly.

QUEVEDO. But he only saw. With his eyes.
And what use are eyes? And through
a telescope. And what's a telescope?
A lens. A distorting lens.
A piece of glass. Look at me. Look.
Look. You see the change?
I have thrown away my glasses.

PABLO. It wasn't you, it was the pirates!

QUEVEDO. Precisely. The pirates. We're so lazy,
we have to be pushed. That's what
pirates are for. Don't you see?
I see better than ever! Imagine.
Looking at the world through discs of
glass. Ridiculous. And I never needed
them. Never needed them at all.

PABLO. You were blind.

QUEVEDO. Precisely. Blind to the harmonies.
The inner harmonies. And deaf, yes,
you're right. Deaf too. I never saw
the web. Never saw it. And it was
left to a woman, to a woman to show me.

PABLO. You've gone mad.

QUEVEDO. No it's the world, Pablo. The world is
mad. Madness incarnate. Total chaos.
Or so it seems. But underneath is the web.
Pablo, I've seen the light.
The light of the world.
The web, the wondrous web.
Everything, Pablo. Everything is interconnected.
Everything.
Even the most disparate of objects,
the most hopelessly contrasting events
...all connect. They all connect.
A puddle, Pablo, a puddle connects with
the stars.

PABLO. How?

QUEVEDO. Exactly. How? That, Pablo, that is the point of
poetry. The object of wit.
To make the connections apparent.
And the greater the disparity, the greater the wit. Then
understanding brings the homage of laughter.

PABLO. I don't understand.

QUEVEDO. You don't understand? Pablo, listen. I call you
a pen.

PABLO. A what?

QUEVEDO. A pen, Pablo. A pen. I know.
The intellect objects. You are not a pen.
You have no feathers. You have no nib.
You are not sharp, you are blunt.
Very blunt. And you do not write.
But, Pablo, but: you speak. You record
events. You tell me your day has been
good. Or perhaps bad. Who cares?
You ate spaghetti. You pen. You
speaking pen. I know. The intellect
objects. Pens do not speak. Pens have
no tongues. But on paper, on paper,
Pablo, a pen can be more eloquent than
silver-tongued Cicero himself.

PABLO. Stop.

QUEVEDO. Yes. The intellect objects. A silver tongue could
   not speak. But think, Pablo, think of the worth of the spoken.
   And so we speak of a ruby tongue.

PABLO. Do we.

QUEVEDO. Yes. Of course. Yours for instance.
   I take it it is red. Or a golden tongue.
   A tongue of diamonds.

PABLO. Shite.

QUEVEDO. Yes. 'Shite' too. We are surrounded
   by metaphors. Hordes of them. They
   overcrowd our wardrobes, they overflow
   from drawers. They drop from the ceiling
   in golden showers, and then they run
   towards us wagging their dear little tails.
   Oh, Pablo, Pablo, my dear friend, we live in
   a labyrinth of connections, trapped like
   flies in a web. And yet we do not
   struggle, for the web upholds us, the
   intellect travels free within its
   boundaries, and wanders amazed in awe and
   in wonder.

PABLO. But what do we do?

QUEVEDO. Do, Pablo, do?

PABLO. Yes.

QUEVEDO. We lose ourselves in contemplation.

   QUEVEDO *loses himself in contemplation. Music.* PABLO
   fidgets.

PABLO. But shouldn't we be doing something? Even if it's
   wrong? Things need doing.

   Shouldn't we at least be conspiring?

QUEVEDO. But, my dear man, whatever for?

PABLO. I thought that was why we came. To save Venice.

   From the Turk.

QUEVEDO. Oh, the Turk. I was forgetting. Yes, yes that was what we said. But tomorrow. We'll do it tomorrow.

PABLO. But this is today. And we've been here for months. And I want to go home.

QUEVEDO. You can't. You don't know the way. Don't worry. Listen. Listen to the harmonies.

PABLO. There's a world out there.

QUEVEDO. Where?

PABLO. And what about the Duke?

QUEVEDO. The Duke?

PABLO. Yes, the Duke. What if he comes? What'll he say?

Enter the DUKE. PABLO *and* QUEVEDO *fall into line.*

DUKE. What indeed, dear Pablo, what indeed? You seem surprised.

PABLO. We are.

DUKE. And what have you been doing?

PABLO. Us?

DUKE. Of course.

PABLO. This and that.

QUEVEDO. Hearing the harmonies.

PABLO. Testing out the ground.

DUKE. I have heard nothing.

PABLO. These days you can never trust the post.

DUKE. You think I have been testing?

PABLO. Oh no.

DUKE. I have been acting.

PABLO. I'm sure.

DUKE. Shall I tell you? Sit.
I was carried by the current to a city by the sea. A sad city.

Factions fight in the streets.
Blood spurts from the fountains.
Thieves ransack the mansions.
Law and order have both completely
disappeared. So what do I do?
I assemble an army.
It is greeted with bullets.
I return the compliment with cannons.
Having crushed criminality, I turn to the
slums. Verminous warrens where vices
breed like rabbits. I erase them.
The prisons overflow with human dregs.
I take up lead, I carry steel, and I
cleanse them. I scour the streets for
catamites and I burn them. Their fat
sizzles and spits in the gutters.
I meet like minds. I meet a man who
has killed four adulterous wives.
I make him Chief of Police.
Together we investigate.
We carry through reforms.
We find methods of interrogation both
slow and inefficient. We improve them.
Soon criminals are hanging with the ink
still wet on their confessions.
People are children. Strictness develops
them. The idle are set to work.
Beggars are banished. I find priests
preaching sedition from the pulpits.
They have forgotten the Gospel.
I cut out their tongues.
I issue a proclamation.
'Citizens of Venice,' I tell them.
They tell me I am in Crete. I hang them.
My work is done. Order has been restored:
the streets are silent.
I leave Crete for Venice.
Citizens bewail my absence.
I harden my heart, I commandeer a
frigate, and hoist up every sail.
We are shipwrecked at the Lido.

> A priest conducts me, I hurry here
> towards you, and what do I find?
> What do I find?

PABLO. Don't tell me. Let me guess.

DUKE. I find you sunk in idleness.
> Submerged in sloth.
> Venice totters on its axis,
> With bated breath the world awaits,
> And you do nothing. Nothing at all.

PABLO. Appearances are deceptive.

DUKE. They had better be.

PABLO. We've been terribly busy.

DUKE. Have you?

QUEVEDO. I have laid the foundations of a new aesthetic.

DUKE. Is that all?

QUEVEDO. Isn't it enough?

PABLO. Don't take any notice. He's joking.

DUKE. Joking?

PABLO. No I mean he's not joking. Not exactly. He knows we cannot talk freely. There are spies everywhere. Be patient. All will be revealed. He'll take you up to his room.

QUEVEDO. What?

PABLO. You will show His Highness your room. He will be interested.

QUEVEDO. Will he?

PABLO. Yes. Fascinated. The strategic situation.

DUKE. Very well.

PABLO. I'll join you later.

QUEVEDO. The view is splendid. The dreaming spires. The bustle on the canal. The human comedy.

Exit QUEVEDO *and the* DUKE.

PABLO. Dukes. Conspirators. Poets. What a nightmare. Who's in charge?

Enter the PRIEST.

PRIEST. May I help?

PABLO. Yes –

PRIEST. You seem concerned.

PABLO. I am. You see, there's this Duke…

PRIEST. I sympathise.

PABLO. He wants a conspiracy. We don't have one. He's angry.

PRIEST. Naturally.

PABLO. And the poet's gone mad.

PRIEST. Had a vision of the truth.

PABLO. I don't see the difference.

PRIEST. Perhaps there is none. Don't worry. All will be well.

PABLO. Will it?

PRIEST. I know your needs. You want a conspiracy? You shall have one. This very night.

PABLO. You're awfully kind.

PRIEST. Think of it as Venetian hospitality. And before the conspiracy, a visit. A special one. In secret.

PABLO. He'll go for that.

PRIEST. Tonight then.

PABLO. Aye, tonight.

PRIEST. By the canal. As the moon rises, the owl will hoot.

The PRIEST *snaps his fingers. The lights dim. Exit the*
PRIEST. PABLO *is impressed. He snaps his fingers. Nothing*
happens. Enter QUEVEDO *and the* DUKE.

DUKE. Are you sure this is the right canal?

QUEVEDO. Of course it's the right canal.

> QUEVEDO *stays in his corner. The* DUKE *goes over to* PABLO.

DUKE. Pablo. What's happened to him?

PABLO. Maybe the water.

DUKE. All he can talk about is Vitruvius. What does that mean?

PABLO. It's a bad sign.

DUKE. And spheres. Some kind of singing spheres. I told him it was just the canal. He said it was subsumed into a greater harmony. I think it's the air. Unhealthy. Of course we'll have it removed.

QUEVEDO. Pablo. What's he saying?

PABLO. He's glad to see you.

QUEVEDO. Poor man. I showed him my window. The most beautiful view in Europe. All he saw were gun emplacements.

DUKE. Pablo. He's talking about me.

PABLO. He's just admiring the view.

DUKE. There isn't a view.

PABLO. Well, you know how he is.

DUKE. We used to talk so well together. The science of war.

> The lives of the generals. Alexander. Julius Caesar. Scipio Africanus. Me.

QUEVEDO. Pablo.

PABLO. Yes.

QUEVEDO. Look at the moon.

PABLO. Which one?

QUEVEDO. There. Look. Just there. The secret of the universe.

PABLO. You sure?

DUKE. Pablo.

PABLO. Coming.

DUKE. Where is that priest?

PRIEST. Behind you. Did I startle you?

DUKE. Not in the least.

PRIEST. Allow me to apologise.

DUKE. Certainly not. Where are the conspirators?

PRIEST. Assembling in their place and time. First we must make a journey. Through danger and darkness to the heart of power.

The PRIEST *snaps his fingers. Lights go out completely.*

PABLO. We'll need some candles.

PRIEST. Of course. Allow me.

Enter SISTER, *who distributes lighted candles.*

QUEVEDO. The flickering lights of faith.

PRIEST. Naturally. Follow me.

The PRIEST *takes them on a conducted tour of the stage. They crawl, skirt invisible obstacles, etc., as appropriate.*

Take care. The doorway is low.

DUKE. The walls seem thick.

PRIEST. We are in the cellars of the palace.

DUKE. Are there any dungeons?

QUEVEDO. The prisons of the intellect.

DUKE. Your prisons are famous. I would be honoured to visit them.

PRIEST. Take care. The oubliette.

DUKE. Is it deep? (*Echo from well: '…eep …eep'.*)

QUEVEDO. Deep as ignorance.

PRIEST. Thirty feet.

DUKE. A bagatelle. In Madrid they are deeper.

PRIEST. The poisoned spike.

QUEVEDO. The barb of malice.

DUKE. Will it kill?

PRIEST. In fifteen seconds.

DUKE. In Madrid they are slower.

PRIEST. The strangling lasso.

DUKE. Where?

PRIEST. Under your feet. One step, there, on that stone, a rope
falls and – (*Strangling sound.*)

DUKE. Most interesting.

PRIEST. You don't have it in Madrid?

QUEVEDO. The stranglehold of lies?

DUKE. Not in Madrid.

PRIEST. Take care. The Ducal sewer.

DUKE (*treads on something*). Yurrccchhh. How dare it?

QUEVEDO. Outside is beauty. Filth and darkness lie within.

PRIEST. We are under the privy.

QUEVEDO. The privy council. The stench of power.

PRIEST. Almost at our destination. Ssshh. We have travelled
through the perils of the path to power. And now we are there.
Hide in the shadows. Don't breathe a word. Behold the Doge.

Enter MR *and* MRS DOGE, *with elaborate robes, carrying
candle lanterns.*

MR DOGE. Are we almost there?

MRS DOGE. I hope so. I think I can see the bed.

MR DOGE. Why can't we have a small bedroom?

MRS DOGE. It wouldn't be right, dear, you know it wouldn't.
I tell you what. We'll stop for a minute and have a little rest.
Here, let me loosen your buckles. There. Isn't that better?

MR DOGE. Oh, what a relief. Turn round and I'll do yours. These damn fasteners. So stiff. There.

MRS DOGE. Oh, that's better.

MR DOGE. My feet are sore.

MRS DOGE. Sit down and I'll give them a rub. There.

MR DOGE. Oooh. What a day.

MRS DOGE. Was it the arsenal again? You've never taken to that place.

MR DOGE. I never have and I never will and there's an end to it. But it makes no difference. I have to go. It's my duty.

MRS DOGE. You've always done your duty. There's not many as can say that.

MR DOGE. Always have and always will. Doesn't stop you wishing, though. I've to wed the sea tomorrow.

MRS DOGE. Tomorrow, is it?

MR DOGE. Same every year. Out I go, in the blazing heat, in that barge. Nothing but a painted bathtub, that's all it is. One day it's going to go straight down to the bottom with me and all the council in it. Maybe not such a bad thing, far as the council is concerned, but I don't want it to happen to me.

MRS DOGE. Quite right, dear.

MR DOGE. But no one takes a blind bit of notice.

MRS DOGE. Still you must admit it's a nice ceremony. I always like the music. They do manage them very well.

MR DOGE. That's as may be, love, but it's not my cup of tea. I mean I just drop a gold ring into the sea and it's meant to be my wife. Doesn't make sense. It's meant to do my bidding. Never does.

MRS DOGE. You've a point there of course.

MR DOGE. I tell them every year. And I told them today. I said, look that ship is rotting on her moorings, rotting away, and that cannon is so rusty you'd think it was underwater and

I promised last year to do something and what have they done? Nothing. They ignored me. So I said, can I go to my garden? But oh no. It was back to the office. Reports from the secret police. This month's victory. This time it's Crete. Plans for the celebration. Receipts for the fireworks. Year in, year out. If this is greatness they can keep it.

MRS DOGE. Well, all we can do is our best.

MR DOGE. If it weren't for you, I don't know how I'd manage.

MRS DOGE. No matter what, we've still got each other.

MR DOGE. Things were better in the old days.
Remember those bean stews?

MRS DOGE. Fresh from the garden.

MR DOGE. You don't get beans like that any more. They look nice and green, but they don't have the taste. If I could just have a decent patch of ground, and a couple of years to work on it.

MRS DOGE. It's no use hankering after what you can't get.

We're Doges for life and we'll just have to lump it.

MR DOGE. If we could only get some sleep.

MRS DOGE. Come on, let's have a go. We've had our rest, and it can't be far to that bed now. Come on. We can take our time. Easy does it. Hold tight. That's the way…

Exeunt DOGES. *The* DUKE *leaps forward.*

DUKE. This is an outrage!

PABLO. I thought it was very sad.

PRIEST. You see? He's seen it. The pathos.

DUKE. Pathos be damned. It's pathetic.

QUEVEDO. The pathetic emptiness of power.

DUKE. You and your damned cynicism.

PABLO. No, I think he's right.

DUKE. Perverting the lower orders! It's shameful. The Doge. Ruler of one of the great states of Europe! An old man. An ordinary dull old man.

PRIEST. Will you not also get old?

DUKE. I doubt it. But I might: I'll concede that, I might. But think of our King. His unquenchable dignity. His courageous defiance of disease. And that is the measure of greatness: the extent to which we overcome. Overcome our human weakness.

Of course.

The PRIEST, PABLO *and* QUEVEDO *blow out candles and exit.*

And that confirms me in my purpose. To overthrow the decrepit state of Venice and replace it with the throne of Spain. The old empire will be reborn.

Where are you?

PRIEST (*a long way offstage*). The conspirators await.

Take care. The lasso.

DUKE. The lasso? Yurchh. The sewer. One false step... Ah. Safe. Now what? The poisoned spike. Fifteen seconds. There. But what next? I've forgotten. The oubliette!

The candle goes out. The sound of a falling DUKE. *The* CONSPIRATORS *and the* PRIEST *rush on in darkness.*

CONSPIRATOR 3. The state is a rotten door.

DUKE. Who's that?

CONSPIRATOR 4. If you don't kick it, it won't fall.

CONSPIRATOR 1. It's the same with sweeping the floor.

CONSPIRATOR 2. Where the broom does not reach...

CONSPIRATOR 4. The dust will not go away by itself.

CONSPIRATOR 3. Are we gathered?

Light goes up on a huddle of CONSPIRATORS, *cloaked and masked, raising their daggers in a spotlight. The* PRIEST *stands apart.*

CONSPIRATORS. We are gathered.

The CONSPIRATORS *crouch down in a huddle.*

DUKE (*sees* PRIEST). What's this?

PRIEST (*motioning him back*). A conspiracy.

The DUKE *withdraws.*

CONSPIRATOR 3. The agenda.

CONSPIRATOR 1 *and* 2 (*raising bottles*). Have some wine.

CONSPIRATOR 3. When you have quite finished.

CONSPIRATOR 4. The agenda.

CONSPIRATOR 1. A toast. Death to the Doge.

ALL. Death to the Doge.

CONSPIRATOR 3. As I was saying. The condition of the people.

CONSPIRATOR 2. Very grave.

CONSPIRATOR 3. As the comrade says, it is very grave.

CONSPIRATOR 4. The people have lost all direction. Bombarded with an incessant barrage of lies, conditioned for work…

CONSPIRATOR 3. Which is denied them.

CONSPIRATOR 2. Yes.

CONSPIRATOR 4. Without direction or hope they drift into prostitution and crime.

CONSPIRATOR 1. Yes. Into crime.

CONSPIRATOR 4. What then, in this grave situation, is the next step?

CONSPIRATOR 2. What is it?

CONSPIRATOR 4. The answer is clear. Re-education.

CONSPIRATOR 3. I disagree.

CONSPIRATOR 4. What?

CONSPIRATOR 3. The priority must lie with the provision of work.

CONSPIRATOR 4. I say education!

CONSPIRATOR 3. You used to say work!

CONSPIRATOR 4. Yes, but I meant *work*!

CONSPIRATOR 1. But, comrades, who wants to work?

CONSPIRATOR 2. Absolutely.

The CONSPIRATORS *confer together. The* DUKE, *dissatisfied, addresses the* PRIEST.

DUKE. This is meant to be a conspiracy.

PRIEST. It is.

DUKE. It's a tea party. A talking shop. Isn't it time for action?

The PRIEST *taps* CONSPIRATOR 3 *on the shoulder.*

CONSPIRATOR 3 (*to* DUKE). The situation is complex. It has to be correctly analysed.

The DUKE, *still dissatisfied, takes* CONSPIRATOR 3 *confidentially off to one side.*

DUKE. Analysed? This is no time for analysis. We must do something. What do you propose?

CONSPIRATOR 3 (*returns to others, raises dagger*). Death to the Doge!

CONSPIRATOR 1. An end to oppression!

CONSPIRATOR 2. A true republic!

CONSPIRATOR 4. Peace and justice!

CONSPIRATORS *drop back into a huddle.*

DUKE (*to* PRIEST). You fool! Took me to the wrong conspiracy. I don't want peace. I don't want justice. I want the rule of law.

The CONSPIRATORS *look up.*

CONSPIRATOR 3. A Spaniard!

DUKE. Yes, a Spaniard. And proud.

CONSPIRATOR 4. The ageing empire.

CONSPIRATOR 3. The most backward state in Europe.

DUKE. The most advanced. The leader of the world.

CONSPIRATOR 2. Yeah?

DUKE. Yes. We are not backward. We invented the stirrup.

CONSPIRATORS *laugh derisively.*

The aqueduct. The cathedral.

CONSPIRATOR 4. The inquisition and the stake.

DUKE. We are Christian, yes.

CONSPIRATOR 3. (*to* PRIEST). I think we should kill him.

CONSPIRATOR 4. Re-educate him.

DUKE. I'd rather die.
You talkers. You dabblers in shopworn theories. You
cowards. You think life is just a matter of debate. Some kind
of sick joke.

CONSPIRATOR 3. I take life very seriously indeed. And I will
take great pleasure in ending yours.

DUKE. That's all you're good for. But I tell you I have changed
the world.

PRIEST. And do you like it any better?

DUKE. That's not the point. I have stamped my mark on the
world. I have won victories. I have conquered cities.

CONSPIRATOR 1 (*to* PRIEST). He killed my son.

CONSPIRATOR 2. He burnt my crops.

CONSPIRATOR 3. He poisoned my wells.

CONSPIRATOR 4. He tortured my friend.

DUKE. I did what I had to. It was nothing personal. I did my duty and now I defy you.

CONSPIRATORS advance on the DUKE. *The* PRIEST *holds them back.*

PRIEST. Wait.

DUKE. What for?

PRIEST. Wait for you to change.

DUKE. You want repentance? Reformation? You're too late. I will never change. I will hold firm to the very end. Firm and resolute.

CONSPIRATOR 1. Stupid. (*Exit.*)

CONSPIRATOR 2. Predictable. (*Exit.*)

CONSPIRATOR 3. Tedious. (*Exit.*)

CONSPIRATOR 4. Cruel. (*Exit.*)

The DUKE *advances on the* PRIEST.

PRIEST. Go away.

The PRIEST *looks at the* DUKE. *The* DUKE *slowly retreats. As he does, enter* PABLO *and* QUEVEDO, *as if pulled on by invisible thread.*

DUKE (*to* QUEVEDO). I blame you for this.
I shouldn't have listened to you.
Should never have set foot in Venice.
Why didn't I stay where I was?
Taking decisions.
Implementing clear-cut policies.
In the daylight.
Under the harsh sun.
And then I left it all,
And entered your damn world of shadows.
Why did I do it? Why did I need you?
But I won't die. You'll see.
You can't kill me.
I won't die. I won't die.

Exit the DUKE.

PRIEST. Did you see? Aren't you glad. Well? You wanted rid of
    him, didn't you? And now he's gone. Celebrate. What's the
    matter with you?

PABLO. But you can't get rid of him that easily.

PRIEST. But I have.

PABLO. He'll come back.

PRIEST. Then let him.

QUEVEDO. My man is right. We should not rejoice. Nothing
    has been won.

PRIEST. Nothing has been lost.

QUEVEDO. But he will come back. He will.

PRIEST. If he must then let him. For now he's gone. Celebrate.

QUEVEDO. Celebrate?

Music and laughter offstage.

PRIEST. Yes.

PABLO. You're joking.

Enter MUSICIAN *and ex-*CONSPIRATORS, *without their
    masks.*

PRIEST. Don't begrudge us our little celebration.
    You must allow us our little festivals.
    You remember the story our teacher told.
    Of the wise man who built his house
    upon the rock and the foolish one who built
    his on the sand? We built ours on the mud.
    We compromised.
    And now we are sinking.
    Year by year the cracks widen in our foundations.
    Year by year the tide water rises.
    Already it has flooded our cellars;
    Soon it will beat against our doors.
    Then the waves will come and wash us from the face of
    the earth.
    The clouds gather. The storm is rising.

And it will come. Nothing can stop it.
We know. We laugh when we can; we live, as we must.
Fear eats away our hearts. Will it spare us,
We wonder, will it spare our children?
Yet what can we do? Tear down our city?
Label the stones and move them, stone by stone,
Rebuild them on the higher ground?
All our energy is taken up with living.
Besides, is there any mountain high enough to hide us,
Is there depth enough in any cave?
I doubt it. Crying is easy, Quevedo,
Laughter requires a little more strength.

The MUSICIAN *starts to play, quietly at first. He and the others move across the stage.* PABLO *hesitates, then goes to join them. They greet him. Music and laughter as they leave. We continue to hear them offstage. The* PRIEST *waits for* QUEVEDO.

Come. Or it will all be over.

QUEVEDO. Is theology a kind of dancing?

PRIEST. A very special kind.

QUEVEDO. I don't know how. Teach me.

The PRIEST *and* QUEVEDO *exit together. Light drains from the stage.*

Offstage, a door slams, and the party is over. The light turns bright and harsh.

QUEVEDO *and* PABLO *are coming back on stage.* PABLO *with cases. They are wearing each other's hats. They squint a bit blearily at the light. They exchange hats.* QUEVEDO *takes out his glasses and tries them on. Then he holds them up and puts them away again. He doesn't need them.* PABLO *takes a swig from a bottle and has a good look round.*

PABLO. Well, we're back. Madrid hasn't changed.

A WOMAN *comes on with a parcel.*

WOMAN. Are you Pablo?

PABLO. Yes.

WOMAN. Something for you.

PABLO. For me? What is it?

WOMAN. You'd better sign for it.

PABLO (*signing*). Right. But what is it?

The WOMAN *goes.* PABLO *unwraps the parcel.*

(*Dismayed.*) It's a baby! Someone's given me a baby!

MARIA (*enters*). Pablo!

PABLO *tries to hide the baby. Then he understands.*

PABLO. Maria! Is this…

MARIA. Ours.

They have a big hug. QUEVEDO *smiles benevolently.*

PABLO. He's lovely.

MARIA. She is, isn't she?

PABLO. Oh, it's a girl. She's beautiful. She's got your eyes.

MARIA. Poor thing. She's got your nose.

They have another cuddle. Enter the DUCHESS.

DUCHESS (*to* QUEVEDO). You're back. You've changed.

QUEVEDO. So have you.

MARIA. What's it like in Venice?

PABLO (*with baby*). Amazing. They have great parties.

QUEVEDO. I've got presents.

He opens the first case, which is full of scarves and silks.

It all comes from China. Across the desert. By camel.

Great excitement. Opens second case.

And there's perfume. And. Best of all.

He opens the third case.

Books. From the new presses. And.

He takes out parcels.

(*To* MARIA.) That's for you. And that's for the baby.

MARIA. But how did you know?

QUEVEDO. I guessed. Poetic intuition.

He carefully hands a third parcel to the DUCHESS.

And that's for you.

DUCHESS. Is it fragile?

Enter the DUKE.

DUKE. I'm back!

The DUCHESS *drops her parcel. A sound of breaking glass. A deathly hush.*

Aren't you pleased to see me?

PABLO. We'd better be going.

They start to pack up all the presents.

DUKE. But I saved Venice.

QUEVEDO (*politely*). Did you?

DUKE. Yes. I fought a horde of pirates. I defied the Doge. I masterminded a conspiracy. I conquered Crete. Where are you going?

The others are beginning to drift offstage.

DUCHESS. Home. It's time to go home.

DUKE. But we must celebrate. A banquet.

DUCHESS. I'm sorry. We had to sell the gold plate. (*Exits.*)

DUKE. Can't we have some music?

MARIA. We sent the orchestra home. (*Exit with* PABLO.)

DUKE. But we must have something. Quevedo, this calls for an epic. In rhyming couplets.

QUEVEDO. I'm sorry. I've got another commission. (*Exits.*)

PABLO *briefly re-enters, still cuddling the baby.*

DUKE. Pablo!

PABLO. Ssssshhh. You'll wake the baby. (*Exits.*)

DUKE. But I saved Venice! We must celebrate. I saved Venice! Doesn't that mean something? Doesn't it?

The light fades.

The play ends.

www.nickhernbooks.co.uk

facebook.com/nickhernbooks

twitter.com/nickhernbooks